"When I'm onstage, I'm out of body. That's what the rehearsals, the practicing, the playing is for. You work to a place where you're all out of body. And that's when something happens. You reach a plane of creativity and inspiration. A plane where every song that has ever existed and every song that will exist in the future is right there in front of you. And you just go with it for as long as it takes."

Prince

1958–2016

Essential Library

An Imprint of Abdo Publishing | abdopublishing.com

PRINCE
MUSICAL ICON
BY STEPHANIE WATSON

CREDITS

abdopublishing.com

Published by Abdo Publishing, a division of ABDO, PO Box 398166, Minneapolis, Minnesota 55439.

Printed in the United States of America, North Mankato, Minnesota
092016
092016

Editor: Elizabeth Dingmann Schneider
Series Design: Becky Daum

Publishers Cataloging-in-Publication Data
Names: Watson, Stephanie, author.
Title: Prince: musical icon / by Stephanie Watson.
Description: Minneapolis, MN : Abdo Publishing, [2017] |
Series: Lives cut short |
Includes bibliographical references and index.
Identifiers: LCCN 2016941963 | ISBN 9781680783643 (lib. bdg.) |
ISBN 9781680795165 (ebook)
Subjects: LCSH: Nelson, Prince Rogers, 1958-2016--Juvenile literature. | Singers--United States--Biography--Juvenile literature. | Rock musicians--United States--Biography--Juvenile literature. |Musicians--United States--Biography--Juvenile literature. | Actors--United States--Biography--Juvenile literature.
Classification: DDC 782.42166092 [B]--dc23
LC record available at http://lccn.loc.gov/2016941963

TABLE OF CONTENTS

1

Super Bowl Superstar

It was halftime at Super Bowl XLI, the February 4, 2007, matchup between the Indianapolis Colts and the Chicago Bears. As rain soaked the crowd of more than 74,000 people watching the game at Miami's Sun Life Stadium, 140 million television viewers also looked on from around the world.

Suddenly, fireworks leapt from the top of the stadium. An explosion of fire erupted in the center of the arena. Then the stage lit up, revealing Prince Rogers Nelson, aka the Artist

▸ Prince delivered a memorable performance at Super Bowl XLI despite facing a powerful rainstorm.

Formerly Known as Prince. The glowing purple stage was in the shape of the unpronounceable symbol Prince had changed his name to in 1993 in the midst of a bitter contract dispute with his record company, Warner Bros. The elusive star, whom music critics have referred to as an "enigma" and a "genius," began playing one of his biggest hits, "Let's Go Crazy."[1]

The 12-minute performance included more of Prince's greatest hits—"1999" and "Purple Rain"—along with covers of songs such as the Foo Fighters' "Best of You" and Creedence Clearwater Revival's "Proud Mary." The show was filled with iconic moments, including Prince's performance of the epic guitar solo from "Purple Rain" in silhouette behind a giant white tarp. "Nearly every Super Bowl since 2007 has owed its jaw-dropping halftime moment to Prince's legacy," wrote one reporter.[2] In 2015, *Billboard* magazine named Prince's performance

The Origins of Prince's Symbol

How did Prince come up with the symbol he used to replace his name? In 1992, when Prince was working on his latest album, he asked designers Mitch Monson and Lizz Luce to create a symbol for the record's title. He wanted the symbol to combine the astrological signs for male and female. "He really wanted to see this feminine quality to [the symbol], and have this mix of male and female," Monson said. "He saw those elements being important, and being integrated."[3] And with that, the famous symbol was born.

▲ Prince performs a guitar solo surrounded by his backup dancers.

the best Super Bowl halftime performance of all time.

This epic moment marked a return for Prince, after his contract dispute and name change had taken him out of the spotlight for more than a decade. Though he had been writing and performing constantly during that time, his decision to release his music under his own label had kept his songs off the charts and kept him out of public view. Years of eccentric behavior, such as changing his name to a symbol and going everywhere with a bodyguard by his side, had alienated him from all but his most loyal fans. Show-stopping performances at the Grammy Awards and Rock and Roll Hall of Fame shows in 2004 finally brought Prince and his music back into the mainstream. The Super Bowl show not only

Make It Rain

February is usually a dry season in Florida. But on the morning of February 4, 2007, Miami found itself in the middle of a downpour. The producers of the Super Bowl XLI halftime show began to panic. The halftime stage included a tile surface that would be very slippery when wet, and Prince was famous for performing in high-heeled shoes. On top of that, his performance would include four separate electric guitars. Producer Don Mischer decided he needed to call his star performer to check in about the weather conditions. He nervously told Prince, "I want you to know it's raining. Are you okay?" There was a pause on the other end of

▲ THE STAGE AT SUPER BOWL XLI WAS IN THE SHAPE OF PRINCE'S FAMOUS SYMBOL AND LIT UP IN HIS SIGNATURE COLOR, PURPLE.

cemented Prince's return to popular music but also confirmed his position as a visionary, pioneer, and legend.

Yet less than a decade after Prince reestablished his supremacy in the music industry, he was gone—dead from an overdose of painkillers at just 57 years old. His fans, fellow musicians, and industry leaders reeled from the loss. How did the rollercoaster of Prince's life and career end so prematurely and tragically?

2

Born to Perform

Prince Rogers Nelson was born on June 7, 1958, at Mount Sinai Hospital in Minneapolis, Minnesota. His parents named him after the jazz group his father, John L. Nelson, performed with: the Prince Rogers Trio. "I named my son Prince because I wanted him to do everything I wanted to do," his father said.[1]

What John wanted to do was be a musician. Yet he couldn't support himself full-time playing piano at clubs. So by day, he worked as a plastic molder for Honeywell Electronics in

▸ As Prince's career took off, he became known for his energetic performance style.

Minneapolis. Prince's mother, Mattie Della Shaw, was a jazz singer who performed with the Prince Rogers Trio. The couple proved that opposites attract. Mattie was wild and outgoing. John was serious and quiet. Yet they shared a love of music, and they would pass that to their son.

Both Mattie and John had children from previous marriages. When Prince was born, he had six half-siblings. John had three daughters, Lorna, Sharon, and Norrine, and two sons, John Jr. and Duane. Mattie had a son named Alfred. In 1960, Prince's sister Tika Evene (Tyka) was born.

Prince's father was originally from Louisiana. He moved to Minneapolis in the 1950s to escape the racism of the South. That was where he and Mattie had met. Minneapolis was almost entirely white. In 1960, African Americans made up only 2 percent of Minneapolis's population.[2] Still, the Nelsons lived in a mostly African-American neighborhood. They

Family Stories

Although both of Prince's parents are African American, when reporters asked him about his heritage, he'd often change his story. A 1981 *Rolling Stone* article reported his father was half-black and his mother was Italian. In other stories, his father was half-Italian and his mother was a mix of ethnicities. Prince said he remained vague about his racial background because, "I wanted people to respect me for my music, not whether I was black or white."[3]

had a modest home in North Minneapolis.

Call Me Skipper

Mattie nicknamed Prince "Skipper" because "he was so small in size and he was just real cute, he was a darling baby," she said.[4] As a child, he preferred to be called Skipper because Prince was his father's stage name.

MUSICAL ORIGINS

When Prince was five years old, his mother took him to see his father perform in a Minneapolis club. As he watched a group of pretty girls dance around his father and heard the audience scream, he decided he wanted to be a musician.

Prince played around on his father's piano at home. He used it to compose his first song, "Funk Machine," at age seven. Whenever his mother took him to the department store, he'd suddenly disappear. She'd find him in the music department, playing whatever instruments they had.

Growing up, Prince listened to many types of music on the radio. Funk musician James Brown and singer-songwriter Joni Mitchell were two of his earliest influences. He also liked Carlos Santana, Sly Stone, Fleetwood Mac, Stevie Wonder, and Jimi Hendrix.

A New School

In 1967, Minneapolis began desegregating its schools. The goal was to give black children the same quality education as white children. That year, Prince was in fifth grade. He and his sister Tyka were bused to John Hay Elementary School in a wealthy white neighborhood. The students there often teased Prince and his sister. Sometimes they called the siblings racist names. "When we had to run to get on the bus, we were chased by people. I thought it was because we were the new kids. I didn't know it was because we were black," Tyka recalled.[7]

A Breakup

By the late 1960s, Mattie and John weren't getting along. They often had loud arguments. John resented having to give up his dream for his wife and kids. "I think music is what broke her and my father up," Prince later said.[5] In 1968, when Prince was ten, his parents divorced.

His father moved into an apartment in downtown Minneapolis. Prince stayed in his mother's home, but he visited his father. To fill the emptiness he felt after the divorce, Prince played the piano his dad had left behind. Mattie remarried Heyward Baker. "I disliked him immediately," Prince said of Baker. "He would bring us lots of presents all the time, rather than sit down and talk with us and give us companionship."[6] Baker and Mattie eventually had a son named Omarr.

School Jam

In 1970, Prince moved in with his father and went to Bryant Junior High near his dad's

▲ PRINCE'S FRESHMAN CLASS PHOTO, 1972–1973

apartment. Prince was smart, but he wasn't very interested in school. He cared more about music than books. By the time he started at Central High School, he had taught himself to play piano, keyboards, and drums. Prince would later reflect, "The key to longevity is to learn every aspect of music that you can."[8] At the time, friends called him the "human jukebox" because he could imitate many popular artists of the time.[9]

▲ AS A TEENAGER, PRINCE LIVED AT THE ANDERSON FAMILY HOME ON RUSSELL AVENUE IN NORTH MINNEAPOLIS.

Prince and friend Andre Simon Anderson decided to start a band. They were called Grand Central. The band included several other members. Andre's younger sister, Linda, played keyboards. Terry Jackson and William Doughty played percussion. And Charles "Chazz" Smith (Prince's cousin) was on drums, although he was later replaced by Morris Day. Prince moved into Andre's house in 1972, and they would practice late into the night.

The band performed covers of popular songs at community centers, the YMCA, and school dances. In 1975, Prince and Grand Central were playing a party in Minneapolis when Pepe Willie saw them perform. Willie, a songwriter, was married to Prince's first cousin Shauntel. Willie decided to manage the band.

Prince Goes Solo

The band, which had now changed its name to Champagne, recorded a demo at Moonsound Studio in Minneapolis in 1976. Prince caught the attention of studio owner and songwriter Chris Moon. "I look out of the control room into the studio, and he's playing the drums," Moon said. "Then I see him wander over and play a bit of piano. And then he stops playing that and picks up the bass."[10] Moon asked Prince to write music to Moon's lyrics. In exchange, he would let Prince record there for free.

That same year, 18-year-old Prince graduated from Central High and devoted himself to

Prince's First Interview

On February 16, 1976, Prince's first interview appeared in his high school newspaper, the *Central High Pioneer*. The story featured a photo of Prince with a big afro, sitting at a piano. Prince told the student reporter that he'd learned to play guitar, bass, keyboards, and drums by ear. He said his band was recording an album that would be released the next summer. Yet he was worried about their ability to make it in Minneapolis. "Mainly because there aren't any big record companies or studios in this state. I really feel that if we would have lived in Los Angeles or New York or

▲ Early in his career, Prince played at small venues such as the Bottom Line in New York City.

writing and recording songs. Moon gave Prince a key to the studio. The fledgling artist would stay there all weekend, sleeping on the studio floor.

In the fall of 1976, Prince left Champagne and went solo. Moon convinced him to drop his last name and be known simply as "Prince." Moon also introduced Prince to Owen Husney, head of a Minneapolis agency that promoted musicians. Husney agreed to sign on as Prince's manager. He was so impressed with Prince that he started a whole new company, American Artists Inc., just to manage him. "His talent was so great that I walked out of my $8 million-a-year business for him," Husney said.[12] American Artists raised $50,000 from investors to buy Prince instruments and an apartment in downtown Minneapolis so he could record his first album. Prince was on his way.

3

Record Deal

During the winter of 1977, Prince recorded his demo album at Sound 80 studio in Minneapolis. Once again, he played every instrument on the album. And true to his mixed musical influences, the album's sound blended jazz, R&B, pop, rock, and funk. To make his new artist seem more mysterious, Prince's manager, Owen Husney, created a demo package that was completely black except for one word: *Prince*.

Now that Prince had a demo, he needed a record company. But getting a meeting with

▸ In 1981, Prince performed at the Ritz in New York City, a venue known for hosting the biggest acts of the era.

record executives wasn't easy. Husney had to lie. He pitted record companies against each other to create demand. For example, he told Warner Bros. that CBS planned to fly Prince out for a meeting and they'd better hurry up and do the same. The record companies bought it. Five of them—Warner Bros., CBS, A&M, RSO, and ABC/Dunhill—set up meetings.

Three companies—CBS, A&M, and Warner Bros.—were interested in signing Prince. Yet there was a catch. Prince insisted on a three-album deal. Most record companies at the time would agree to only two albums with a new artist. Prince also wanted to produce his own albums. The record companies weren't eager to turn over the reins to an unproven 19-year-old performer. After much negotiating, Warner Bros. finally agreed to the terms. On June 25, 1977, they signed a three-album contract for a total of $180,000. Prince got $80,000 upfront. It was a huge deal for an unknown artist.

Recording Sessions

Warner let Prince produce his first album with one condition. He'd need someone experienced by his side. Tommy Vicari, a veteran engineer who had worked with artists such as Carlos Santana and Billy Preston, came on board.

Prince watched Vicari intently as they worked. He learned how to produce a record from scratch, layering drums, keyboards, bass, and guitar tracks to build a complex sound. Prince picked up these new techniques from Vicari, but his talent was innate. "He seemed to be one of these guys who could hear the entire song in his head, before he even played it," said assistant engineer Steve Fontano.[1]

Practical Joker

In the studio, Prince was serious and focused. Outside of work, he was more fun. He became known among friends as a practical joker. When one of his idols, Chaka Khan, was in San Francisco, California, for a concert, he called her hotel room and pretended to be Sly Stone, the lead singer of Sly and the Family Stone. He invited Chaka Khan to meet him at the studio where he was working. When Khan learned she had been tricked, she was irritated. But she stayed in the studio to hear Prince play. It was the start of a long friendship.

FOR YOU

In February 1978, Prince's first album was finally finished. *For You* went way over budget at a cost of $150,000. It was almost as much money as Warner had committed to all three albums.

Prince produced, composed, arranged, and performed every song on the album. He also played every instrument—all 23 of them. When the album came out in April, reviews were mainly good. Critics compared Prince to Stevie Wonder and Michael Jackson. Yet the album didn't

The Price of Fame

With the release of his first album, *For You,* Prince started to get noticed—especially by a teenage audience. In June 1978, 3,000 screaming fans mobbed him at a North Carolina record store. Prince was naturally reserved, and he was uncomfortable with the attention.

produce a hit. Its first single, "Soft and Wet," only reached Number 21 on the R&B chart and Number 163 on the Pop chart. Prince blamed his manager for the disappointing sales. He and Husney soon parted ways.

A Tour Needs a Band

Warner wanted Prince to go on tour to promote his new album. To perform live, he needed a band. Prince's plan was to recruit a mix of white and black musicians to appeal to a wider audience. So he held auditions. By November, the band had come together. Gayle Chapman and Matt Fink played keyboards. Childhood friend Andre (now known as André Cymone) was on bass. Dez Dickerson played guitar, and Bobby Rivkin (Bobby Z) handled drums. Prince was a perfectionist, and he worked his musicians hard. "We rehearsed until we could do it in our sleep," Rivkin said.[2]

The band debuted on January 5, 1979. They performed in front of 300 people at the Capri Theater in North Minneapolis. Local DJ Kyle Ray introduced Prince as "the next Stevie Wonder."[3] Despite Prince's star potential, he

▲ PRINCE, *CENTER*, HIRED SEVERAL MUSICIANS FROM HIS HOMETOWN TO PLAY IN HIS TOURING BAND, INCLUDING DEZ DICKERSON, *RIGHT*, AND ANDRÉ CYMONE, *LEFT*.

looked unpolished. He was so nervous that he played with his back to the audience. Yet his potential was undeniable. Warner executive Carl Scott called the show "unbelievable."[4]

PRINCE

Prince recorded his self-titled second album, *Prince*, in just 30 days. It cost $35,000—approximately one-fifth of what he'd spent on *For You*. With the less-than-stellar sales of his first album, Prince knew he needed a hit this time.

He got what he wanted. The dance track "I Wanna Be Your Lover" went to Number One on the Soul chart and Number 11 on the Pop chart in the summer of 1979. By March 1980, *Prince* became a gold album with 500,000 copies sold. *Rolling Stone*'s reviewer called his voice "the most thrilling R&B falsetto since Smokey Robinson."[5]

Prince was beginning to look and sound like a star. "The best way to describe Prince was that he had an aura," said Warner Bros. executive Marylou Badeaux.[6] His hair was styled into waves. He took the stage wearing striking clothing, such as skin-tight gold spandex pants, a big puffy shirt, and gold boots.

On the Road with Rick James

Prince got a new manager, Steve Fargnoli. "Steve was one of a tiny handful of people that Prince really trusted," Badeaux said.[7] In 1980, Fargnoli put Prince on tour as the opening act for R&B star Rick James. It wasn't long before Prince was upstaging the headliner.

James wasn't happy with his up-and-coming opening act. He complained that Prince was stealing his look and sound. "Prince was emulating my mic moves. . . . He was calling out my funk chants and even flashing my funk sign,"

▲ PRINCE BECAME KNOWN FOR HIS UNIQUE STYLE IN THE 1980S.

James wrote in his autobiography, *Glow*.[8] The two would remain rivals for years to come.

DIRTY MIND

In October 1980, Prince's third album, *Dirty Mind*, was released. The music had an edgy

The Rebels

In 1979, Prince launched the first of many side projects—a band called the Rebels. The trio was made up of Prince, Dez Dickerson, and André Cymone. Their sound was gritty compared to Prince's own albums. "He wanted to try this punk/rock/new wave thing with the Rebels because he was too afraid to do that within the 'Prince' realm," keyboardist Matt Fink said. "It was an experiment."[10] The Rebels recorded nine songs, but they disbanded before the album was released. The punk/new wave sound they created would inspire Prince's 1980 *Dirty Mind* album.

punk/new wave feel. Most of the lyrics were about sex. On the cover was a photo of Prince wearing only black brief underwear and black stockings under a trench coat. "When I brought it to the record company it shocked a lot of people," Prince said.[9] Still, they didn't make him change the cover—or the lyrics.

Many radio stations thought *Dirty Mind* was too risqué to play on the air. Some record stores wouldn't even put it on their shelves because of the racy cover. But critics loved it. *Rolling Stone*'s reviewer gave it four and a half out of five stars. The *Village Voice* put it on its Top Ten albums list for the year.

Prince's dirty lyrics, sexy outfits, and onstage antics upset keyboardist Gayle Chapman, who was deeply religious. She left the band in 1980. Prince replaced her with 19-year-old Lisa Coleman.

Prince and his band went on tour in the summer and fall of 1981. Their audiences at the time were almost entirely black. In early October, they opened up for legendary rock band the Rolling Stones. One hundred thousand people—most of them white—filled the Memorial Coliseum in Los Angeles, California. Prince's music was very different from what the audience expected to hear at a Rolling Stones concert, and they pelted Prince with oranges, tomatoes, and chicken parts. They booed him off the stage two shows in a row. The Stones tour was the last time Prince would open for any other act.

Onscreen Antics

In 1980, *American Bandstand* was one of the most popular and influential television shows among teenagers. An appearance on the show could instantly send a new artist's record soaring up the charts. Yet when Prince went on the show on January 26, he had an attitude. He barely spoke to host Dick Clark, giving mostly one-word answers during his two-minute interview. When Clark asked how many years earlier Prince had made his demo tape, Prince held up four fingers. To a question about how many instruments he played, Prince coyly responded, "A thousand."[11] Prince's band later revealed he had told them he was going to be a tough interview. "He knew that he wasn't going to suck up to Dick Clark and act like other idiots that go on that show," Bobby Z said.[12]

The Time

In the spring of 1981, Prince launched another musical project. He transformed a local

▲ MORRIS DAY PERFORMS WITH THE TIME.

Minneapolis band named Flyte Tyme into the Time. His former drummer, Morris Day, became the band's lead singer.

The Time showed another side of Prince's personality. They were fun, funky, and filled with attitude. The band's six members wore old-fashioned suits accented with skinny ties. Prince wrote and produced all six songs on their debut album, *The Time*. To hide his involvement,

Prince credited himself on the album under the pseudonym Jamie Starr.

CONTROVERSY

Prince's own next album, *Controversy*, explored broader themes than sex and love. His lyrics covered religion, racism, politics, and current events. He discussed the recent killing of John Lennon, formerly of the band the Beatles, and the murders of children in Atlanta, Georgia. The album reached Number 21 on the *Billboard* Albums chart and went gold.

To promote *Controversy*, Prince launched his first big solo tour. The Time played as his opening act. His solo tour allowed him to draw in his own fans, which were a different crowd from the Rolling Stones fans who had so recently booed him. Prince played large amphitheaters in front of thousands of people. His over-the-top set cost $45,000. It featured a two-tier stage with a fireman's pole Prince slid down. The tour ran from the winter of 1981 to the spring of 1982.

Prince was barely in his 20s, but he had already released four albums and launched a successful headlining tour. He was about to put out a record that would change the course of his career.

4

Rising Star

When Prince began work on his fifth album, he was just 23 years old. Yet his talent and songwriting ability far surpassed his years. "I felt this was his best time," said engineer Peggy McCreary. "He was just on and had so much coming out of him."[1] He recorded part of *1999* in the basement studio of his new home near Lake Minnetonka, just outside of Minneapolis. The other part he recorded at Sunset Sound studio in Los Angeles. Prince worked on the new songs around the clock. He'd go for days without sleep.

▸ Prince often recorded his music in his own studios, such as the ones at his Paisley Park estate.

Prince produced so many songs—70 minutes' worth—that he wanted to make a double album. Because he still wasn't a big star, Warner didn't want to spend the money for two records. Fargnoli, his manager, had to convince them to put out *1999* as a two-album set.

Released in October 1982, the album took a serious theme—the threat of nuclear annihilation—and set it to a dance beat. On its title track, "1999," Prince sings about partying while the world ends. *Rolling Stone* magazine gave *1999* four stars and later called it "one of his most influential albums."[2] The single "1999" rose to Number 44 on the *Billboard* Hot 100 chart. It seemed Prince had a hit. But just as quickly as it had risen, the song dropped back down the chart.

Vanity 6

In 1980, Prince met 22-year-old Canadian singer and model Denise Matthews at the American Music Awards. Soon after, they started dating. Prince had been thinking about forming an all-girl group. He made Matthews the act's lead singer. "He told me he was going to make me a star," she said.[3] Prince renamed Matthews "Vanity" and called the band Vanity 6.

Video Launched the Radio Star

Prince's album needed a boost. It got that boost from a brand-new television network, MTV. Short for Music Television, MTV played music videos 24 hours a day, seven days a week. The network launched on August 1, 1981, and it quickly gained a following among teenagers.

In 1982, MTV videos were almost all by white artists and bands, such as Billy Joel, Toto, Pat Benatar, and Duran Duran. Michael Jackson was one of the only black artists who got any airtime. Prince helped break the color barrier in late 1982 when MTV started playing the video for "1999." In 1983, it also played "Little Red Corvette," his second single off the *1999* album. Prince's shiny purple trench coat and pop/funk/R&B sound made him stand out. Soon his videos were on heavy MTV rotation, and he was reaching a much bigger audience. The publicity bumped "1999" into the Top Ten on the *Billboard* Hot 100 chart.

During this period, Prince's band went through a few more changes. Dickerson left to work on his own material. Coleman's friend, 19-year-old Wendy Melvoin, took over on guitar and backup vocals. The lineup was now Melvoin,

Prince Gets a Bodyguard

With Prince's fame came a need for more security. In 1982, he hired former pro wrestler Charles "Big Chick" Huntsberry to be his bodyguard. Huntsberry was an intimidating figure. He stood 6 feet 6 inches tall, weighed more than 300 pounds (140 kg), and had a bushy white beard. At first, Prince's band was terrified of him. "We were on the bus, and no one would even sit near him," Dickerson recalled.[4]

Coleman, Matt Fink ("Dr. Fink"), Mark Brown ("BrownMark"), and Bobby Z. In 1982, Prince gave his band an official name—the Revolution.

1999 TOUR

The tour to promote *1999* started in November 1982 in Chattanooga, Tennessee. Prince performed on a set that was even bigger and more dramatic than the one on his last tour. It had a hydraulic platform and catwalks. Prince had already proven himself as a songwriter, musician, and producer. On stage he showcased his talent as a performer. He did splits in midair. He slid down a pole. And he did all of these feats while singing and playing guitar.

The Time and Vanity 6 opened for Prince on the *1999* tour. Tensions quickly grew between the two bands and their mentor. Members of the Time were bitter

The Color Purple

By the early 1980s, Prince had begun adopting his signature color. He wore a purple coat in his concerts and videos. His album cover and house were both purple. And his next record would have the word *purple* in the title.

Why did he choose purple? It was the color of his hometown football team, the Minnesota Vikings. His idol, Jimi Hendrix, had a hit song called "Purple Haze." Purple symbolizes mystery, creativity, and ambition. Prince became known for all these traits. Yet Prince said his real fascination with the color had to do with the Apocalypse. The color purple made him think of red blood in a blue sky. He pictured the two colors blending together to make purple. He mentioned purple in his end-of-the-world song, "1999."

▲ PRINCE'S HIGHLY ACTIVE PERFORMANCE STYLE SOMETIMES INVOLVED LYING DOWN ON THE STAGE DURING A SHOW.

because they earned only $140 a week, and they had very little control over their own music. In their frustration, they tried to upstage Prince and the Revolution at their own shows. On some nights, the Time was so good they got even bigger applause than the headliner. "The audiences went wild for them," Fink said. "Prince felt we weren't garnering the same response, and it hurt him."[5]

Tensions with Vanity 6 were also high. This was likely because Prince was dating two members of the band—Vanity and Susan Moonsie—at the same time. "And the girls all had to ride on the same bus so it was pretty frightening," a crew member said.[6]

The two opening acts also resented Prince's attitude. Prince was now a big star, and he was acting the part. In March 1983, his tour buses stopped to eat at a roadside restaurant after a concert in Kalamazoo, Michigan. The Time, Vanity 6, and the Revolution all ate together. Prince sat way

The Prince and Michael Jackson Rivalry

In 1983, Prince began making his mark on the music charts. But another young artist had already staked his claim as the king of American pop music. Michael Jackson's *Thriller* album came out a month after *1999*. While *1999* sold 3 million copies, *Thriller* sold 40 million. *1999* had two Top Ten hits ("Little Red Corvette" and "Delirious"). *Thriller* had seven hits.

A rivalry developed between Prince and Jackson. On a few occasions, Prince seemed to show up Jackson. In 1983, Jackson and Prince were both in the audience during a James Brown concert at the Beverly Theater in Los Angeles. Brown invited Jackson to come onstage and perform with him. After Jackson sang and showed off his James Brown dance moves, he insisted Brown invite Prince onstage. Prince arrived, carried on Big Chick's huge shoulders. His dance moves and ripping guitar solo got even bigger cheers than Jackson's across the room with his bodyguard, Big Chick. "It just seemed to be accepted that he was so brilliant and important that he couldn't consort with mere mortals," commented rock journalist Barney Hoskyns.[7] By the time the tour ended in April 1983, Prince had pulled the Time from the bill and Vanity 6 had quit.

The year 1983 marked a huge milestone for Prince. *1999* sold its first 1 million copies and went platinum. The tour earned nearly $10 million, making it one of the highest grossing tours of the year. *Rolling Stone* wrote of Prince, "There just don't seem to be any bounds to Prince's nerve or talent."[8]

5

Purple Reign

Never content to rest on his successes, Prince started to think about his next project while his *1999* tour was still on the road. He carried around a purple notebook and jotted down ideas for a film. "I want to star in the movie," Prince told his managers. "I want my name above the title and I want it to be at a major studio."[1]

Prince had lofty goals, but Warner Bros. knew that producing a movie would cost millions of dollars. It worried about risking that much money on someone who had never made a

▸ In the 1980s, Prince reached new levels of fame and success.

film, much less acted in one. Prince's managers shopped the idea around to a few studios. All of them said no. Finally, Warner Bros. chairman Mo Ostin decided to put his trust in Prince. Ostin gave him $4 million to make the movie he envisioned.

From *Dreams* to *Purple Rain*

Television writer and producer William Blinn signed on to write the movie, which would be loosely based on Prince's life. Blinn had worked on a few popular television shows in the 1970s and early 1980s, including *Fame*, *Starsky and Hutch*, and *Eight Is Enough*. He came to Minneapolis to write the screenplay with Prince, but he found the star difficult to work with. Prince would schedule meetings with Blinn only to cancel them. Finally, Blinn had had enough. "Look, I want out of this," he told Prince's manager, Fargnoli. "I know he's very gifted, but frankly, life's too short."[2]

Prince convinced Blinn to stay on. Blinn finished a first draft of the script based on stories Prince had told him about his musician father. Yet the screenplay he wrote was much darker than Prince's real life. In it, Prince's character was called "the Kid." His father and mother had died in a murder-suicide. (Prince's real parents were very

▲ PRINCE, *RIGHT*, STARRED IN HIS FIRST MOVIE ALONGSIDE APOLLONIA KOTERO, *LEFT*.

much alive.) Blinn called the movie *Dreams*, but about halfway through the second draft, Prince decided he wanted the word *purple* in the title. Blinn thought it was a strange request, but he agreed when he realized how important the color was to Prince.

Before he could finish writing the script, Blinn was called back to Hollywood to work on the third season of *Fame*. Young screenwriter Albert Magnoli was hired to finish the project, which was now titled *Purple Rain*. Magnoli's script was much lighter. It centered on a rivalry between the Kid and another band (played by the Time) at a Minneapolis club. There was also a romance between the Kid and an aspiring singer. Vanity was slated to play the singer. But after a disagreement over money and a breakup with Prince, she dropped out of the project. Auditions were held in Los Angeles and New York, and Prince discovered Vanity's replacement—a 22-year-old actress and model named Patricia Kotero. He called her "Apollonia."

By the time shooting on the film started in November 1983, Prince had prepared by taking dance and acting classes. Each day he arrived at the set on time. He always knew his lines by heart.

Most of *Purple Rain* was shot around Minneapolis. The music scenes were filmed at First Avenue, the club where Prince often performed in the

First Avenue

First Avenue, originally called the Depot, opened on April 3, 1970, at the corner of First Avenue and Seventh Street in Minneapolis. In the 1970s, First Avenue showcased rock, blues, and R&B acts such as Ike and Tina Turner, Chubby Checker, B. B. King, and Rod Stewart. Prince often played there when he was starting out. It was where he launched the "Minneapolis sound," which was the mixture of funk, rock, synth, and new wave he pioneered. First Avenue continues to welcome a diverse range of musical acts.

early 1980s. Six hundred extras were brought in to play the audience.

During filming, Prince also recorded the *Purple Rain* soundtrack. The first single, "When Doves Cry," was released before the movie, on May 16, 1984. The song had an experimental sound, even for Prince. There was no bass track. On the vocals, Prince screamed as if he were in pain. But listeners loved it. "When Doves Cry" spent five weeks at Number One on the Pop chart. The second single, "Let's Go Crazy," also went to Number One. When the *Purple Rain* album hit record stores in June, it sold 2.5 million copies before the movie was even released. It stayed at Number One for 24 weeks and went on to sell 10 million copies.

THE PREMIERE

Purple Rain premiered on July 27, 1984. MTV covered the event live from Mann's Chinese Theatre in Los Angeles. A line of traffic stretched two blocks, as fans tried to catch a glimpse of Prince and other celebrities who attended the premiere, including Eddie Murphy, Quincy Jones, and Kevin Bacon. The crowd screamed, "We love Prince!" as the star pulled up in a purple limo.[3] He wore a purple trench coat and carried a purple flower.

The post-premiere party was held at the nearby Palace Theatre. The room was decorated entirely in Prince's signature color. Flowers, tablecloths, and balloons were all purple. Similar to the premiere, the after party was a star-studded event. Director Steven Spielberg and singers Lionel Richie and John Cougar Mellencamp were there. Prince played three songs for the crowd, but he preferred to stay backstage for the rest of the party.

Some critics thought the writing and acting in *Purple Rain* paled in comparison to the soundtrack. Vincent Canby of the *New York Times* called it "the flashiest album cover ever to be released as a movie."[4] Others thought it was remarkable. The *Los Angeles Herald* declared it "the best rock movie ever made."[5] Fans couldn't get enough of the film. *Purple Rain*, which had cost just over $7 million to make, grossed more than $68 million. While many artists would have celebrated this kind of success, Prince worried he'd reached his peak. "We looked around and I knew we were lost," he said. "There was no place to go but down."[6]

Epic Concert Tour

In November, Prince and the Revolution launched a tour to support *Purple Rain*. If his

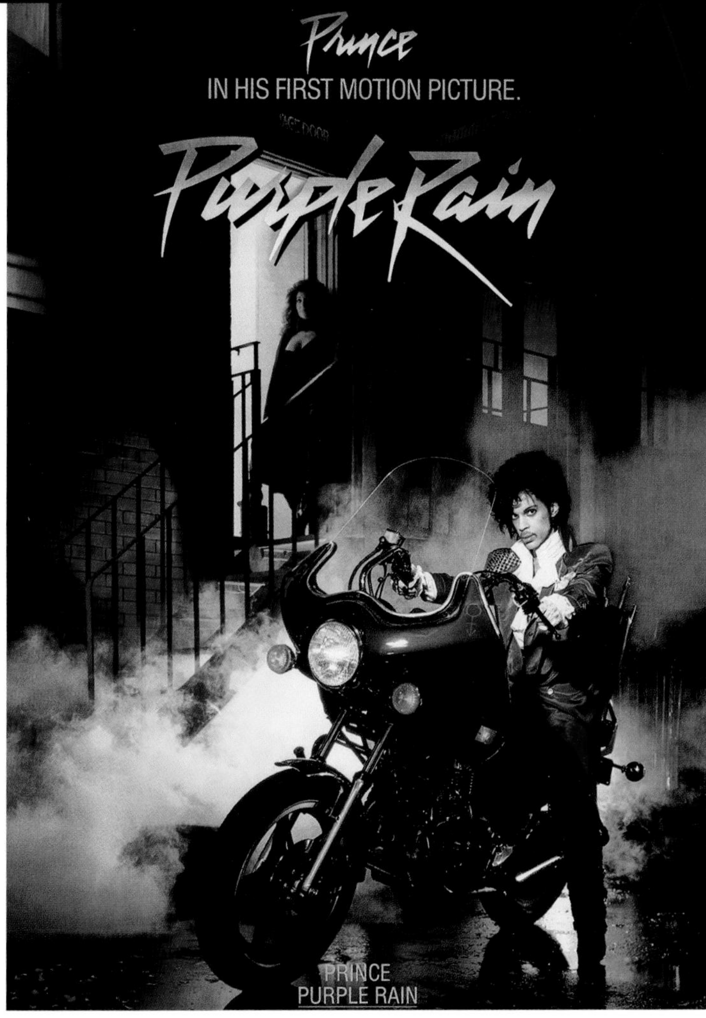

▲ THE MOVIE POSTER FOR *PURPLE RAIN* FEATURED PRINCE'S NAME ABOVE THE TITLE, JUST AS HE HAD ENVISIONED IT.

earlier shows were theatrical, this one was even more spectacular. The set featured lasers, a dry ice machine, and a purple bathtub that rose from beneath the stage. It cost $300,000 and took a crew of 125 people to set up. Prince played 125 concerts in 90 cities. The venues were huge—some could hold as many as 50,000 screaming fans. Prince's core audience had grown. It had also shifted demographically. His earlier audiences had been mostly black. Now, because of MTV and *Purple Rain*, his fans were mainly white.

Awards Season

At the American Music Awards on January 28, 1985, Prince stole the night. He won Favorite Black Album (*Purple Rain)*, Favorite Black Single ("When Doves Cry"), and Favorite Pop/Rock Album (*Purple Rain)*, beating out even Michael Jackson's multiplatinum record, *Thriller*.

Prince's winning streak continued

The Glamorous Life

Prince had already mentored several music acts, including the Time and Vanity 6. In 1984, he wrote and produced an album for an up-and-coming percussionist, Sheila E. Sheila is the daughter of Pete Escovedo, a drummer who played with Santana. She met Prince in 1978 when she went backstage at one of his early shows. When she introduced herself, Prince surprised her by saying, "I know who you are. I've been following your career for a long time. You're an amazing drummer and percussionist."[7]

Prince convinced Sheila E. to launch a career as a solo artist. She reluctantly agreed. The title track from her 1984 debut album, *The Glamorous Life*, went to Number One on the US *Billboard* Dance chart. Sheila opened for Prince during his *Purple Rain* tour. They later dated and fell in love. Prince proposed to her during his at the Grammy Awards, held in February. He walked away with three awards. In March, he followed up those wins with an Oscar for the *Purple Rain* score.

Prince and the PMRC

In December 1984, Tipper Gore, wife of then-Senator Al Gore, bought a copy of *Purple Rain* for her 11-year-old daughter. She was shocked by the sexual lyrics, especially in the song "Darling Nikki." Tipper joined up with several other women in Washington, DC, and formed the Parents Music Resource Center, or PMRC, to fight back against music they found objectionable. Its list of the Filthy 15 included songs by Prince, Madonna, Def Leppard, and Judas Priest. After a Senate hearing in September 1985, the recording industry agreed to start putting a black-and-white warning label on albums that contain potentially objectionable content. The label states: "Parental Advisory: Explicit Content."

His Royal Badness

Even as Prince's popularity grew, he became more isolated and withdrawn. "He just kind of shut himself off," said set designer Roy Bennett. "He became a different person at that point. Between Prince and everyone else, a wall came up."[8] Big Chick was guardian of that wall. He wouldn't let anyone close to Prince—not even his bandmates. The media and public started to view Prince as strange and reclusive. The press nicknamed him "the Purple Pain" and "His Royal Badness."[9]

Prince's image didn't improve after an incident on January 28, 1985. Prince was asked to participate in the recording of "We Are the World" along with other popular artists, including Stevie Wonder, Lionel Richie, Michael Jackson, and Bruce Springsteen. The song would benefit famine victims in Ethiopia and become part of a charity album called *USA for Africa: We Are the World.*

Prince was a no-show. He hadn't wanted to sing on the track and had instead offered to play guitar, but the producers had turned down that offer. Instead of going to the session, he went to a Carlos 'n' Charlie's Mexican restaurant on Sunset Boulevard in Los Angeles. When a photographer tried to climb into Prince's limo to snap a picture of him leaving the restaurant, one of Prince's bodyguards dragged him out of the car and was later arrested for battery. "[He] was being portrayed in the papers as someone who was mean and didn't want to give to the starving, and had his bodyguards beating people up," said Bennett.[10]

Big Chick Sells His Story

On May 7, 1985, an article about Prince appeared in tabloid newspaper the *National Enquirer*. The story portrayed Prince as an eccentric recluse who lived in a walled-off mansion. Prince learned Big Chick had sold the story to the *Enquirer* for $3,000 to pay for drugs. Though Prince was upset, he quickly forgave his friend. "I think they just took everything he said and blew it up," he told *Rolling Stone*.[11] When Big Chick died in 1990, Prince held a benefit concert and raised $60,000 to help his former bodyguard's widow and children.

Yet Prince wasn't heartless. He donated his own original song, "4 the Tears in Your Eyes," to the *We Are the World* album. Prince did other charity work, too—such as giving a free concert for children with disabilities at the Santa Monica Civic Auditorium. Over the years, Prince provided funding for many different charitable organizations, although he preferred to keep his contributions anonymous whenever possible.

SHOW'S OVER

After a hugely successful movie, soundtrack, and tour, Prince was burned out. "I was doing the 75th *Purple Rain* show, doing the same thing over and over," he said. "And I just lost it."[12]

In early April 1985, Fargnoli announced that the star would perform one last show at the Orange Bowl stadium in Miami. It would be his final live appearance for an "indeterminate number of years." Fargnoli said Prince told him he planned to "look for the ladder."[13] What did he mean? Was Prince retiring from music at just 27 years old?

6

HIGHS AND LOWS

Although he'd stopped touring, Prince had no plans to retire. He was still working as hard as ever. While the *Purple Rain* album topped the music charts, he went to work on his next record, *Around the World in a Day*. Again, Prince experimented with a new sound. This time he was influenced by 1960s rock. He incorporated instruments such as the flute, violin, and darbuka, a Moroccan drum. The *New York Times* compared *Around the World in a Day* to 1960s rock icons such as the Beatles, David Bowie,

▸ SOME OF PRINCE'S WARDROBE CHOICES, SUCH AS HIS RUFFLED SHIRTS, WERE SIMILAR TO FASHIONS OF THE 1960S.

and Prince's idol, Jimi Hendrix. The cover paid tribute to the cartoonish landscape on the front of the Beatles' 1969 *Yellow Submarine* album.

Around the World in a Day also marked a new closeness between Prince and his father, who wrote a few of the songs. Their relationship had been strained for many years. "This was the time when he was beginning to bring his father into his life, so his dad was around a lot," said sound engineer Susan Rogers.[1]

When the record was released in April 1985, Prince again wanted to play by his own rules. Normally, record companies would send a single to radio stations for them to play. Prince didn't want *Around the World in a Day* to be commercial. "I was making something for myself and my fans, and the people who supported me through the years," he said.[2] His idea was to send radio stations the whole album and let the DJs play whatever song they chose. Warner wasn't happy, but again they let Prince get his way.

"Raspberry Beret" got more airplay than any other song on the album, so it became the single. Despite a lack of traditional publicity, *Around the World in a Day* sold 3 million copies in the United States. The album stayed at Number One for three weeks.

UNDER THE CHERRY MOON

Given the success of *Purple Rain*, Warner Bros. easily agreed to give Prince $10 million for his next movie, *Under the Cherry Moon*. The story centered on a piano-playing con man named Christopher Tracy (played by Prince) who tries to trick an heiress out of her inheritance. Prince wanted the movie to look and feel like a 1940s-era light romantic comedy.

Prince in Love

Prince had many romances over the years, including with his protégées Vanity, Susan Moonsie, and Sheila E. One of his greatest loves was Susannah Melvoin, his backup singer and the twin sister of band member Wendy Melvoin. When they met in the early 1980s, Prince was totally smitten. He sent Susannah flowers every day for nearly a year. He also wrote several songs for her. One of the most famous was "Nothing Compares 2 U," which Sinead O'Connor made a hit in 1990.

The drama began before the film even started shooting. Prince wanted Madonna to star as the female lead, Mary Sharon. He'd liked her work in the 1985 movie *Desperately Seeking Susan*. She turned him down. Prince's girlfriend, Susannah Melvoin, got the role. But when it became obvious that Susannah couldn't act, British actress Kristin Scott Thomas took over.

Once again, Prince clashed with Warner Bros. Warner didn't like that Prince's character died at the end of the movie. They wanted a happy ending. Prince wanted to shoot the film in black and white. Warner wanted to film in color to make the movie look up-to-date. Although Prince refused to change the ending, he did compromise on the movie's look. It was shot in color and then processed in sepia tones to make it look old-fashioned.

Music video director Mary Lambert was hired to direct the film, but Prince argued with her over the direction of the movie. Prince fired her and then took over as director, though he had never directed a movie. His inexperience showed in the final product. When *Under the Cherry Moon* was released in July 1986, it was widely considered a flop. "Most of the scenes are so awkward, so hopelessly inept that the whole affair looks like a student film that somehow inherited a multimillion-dollar budget," wrote a *Los Angeles Times* reviewer.[3]

Critics were much kinder to the soundtrack, *Parade*. One called the single, "Kiss,"

Win a Date with Prince

To promote *Under the Cherry Moon*, Warner Bros. decided to hold a contest. The 10,000th caller to an MTV contest line would win a date to the premiere with Prince in the winner's hometown. Lisa Barber, a motel chambermaid from Sheridan, Wyoming, was the lucky winner. On July 1, 1986, Prince pulled up in front of her house in a white Buick convertible. Prince put his arm around Barber as they sat in the back row of the theater. Afterward, he and his band performed at the Holiday Inn—the only local venue big enough to stage a concert.

"one of the greatest songs in the history of pop music."[4] Yet it almost didn't get onto the record. Warner didn't like the sound, which features Prince's falsetto vocals over a hypnotic drum beat. "We can't put this out," an executive said. "There's no bass and it sounds like a demo."[5] Prince once again persevered, and "Kiss" went to Number One on *Billboard*'s Hot 100 list.

SIGN O' THE TIMES

By late 1985, band members Melvoin and Coleman were growing dissatisfied. They wanted more creative input into the music. Prince tried to please them by featuring their talents on a new album titled *Dream Factory*. Yet as tensions rose with his band, he scrapped the project.

In August and September, Prince and the Revolution launched a tour throughout Europe and Japan. "It was the best tour we ever did," said Bobby Z.[6] Still, it was the beginning of the end for the Revolution. When the band returned to the United States, Prince fired Melvoin and Coleman. BrownMark quit. "I felt we all needed to grow," Prince said. "We all needed to play a wide range of music with different types of people. Then we could all come back eight times as strong."[7] Melvoin and Coleman remained bitter about the split for many years.

▲ Wendy Melvoin, *right*, and Lisa Coleman, *left*, went on to form their own band called Wendy and Lisa.

Now on his own, Prince began work on his ninth album, *Sign O' the Times*. As usual, he'd produced more songs than the record could hold. He told Warner Bros. he wanted a three-album set. Warner would only allow him to produce a double album. Prince argued, but he finally gave in and cut it down to a double album.

The album included hit singles such as "U Got the Look" and "I Could Never Take the Place of Your Man." Several songs on *Sign O' the Times* tackle some of the decade's biggest issues, such as AIDS, crack cocaine, guns, crime, and nuclear war. They address those themes in many different styles, including funk, gospel, dance, and romantic ballads. Critics hailed the album's technical skill.

The Black Album

While Prince recorded *Sign O' the Times*, he was quietly at work on another experimental album. *The Black Album* features a totally black cover. Prince's name isn't even on it. Warner produced more than 400,000 copies in 1987. It released only a limited number when Prince changed his mind. He asked Warner to destroy the rest. "I could feel this wind and I knew I was doing the wrong thing," he said.[9] Years later, copies of *The Black Album* were so rare they sold for as much as $10,000.

Paisley Park Studios

By 1987, Prince had released nine albums and two movies. He'd created a musical empire. Now he needed a place to house it. Prince decided to build a complex where he could fully explore his creativity.

He chose to locate his studio in Chanhassen, Minnesota, a suburb approximately 20 miles (30 km) southwest of Minneapolis. Prince designed the 65,000-square-foot (6,000 sq m), $10 million complex with the help of California architect Bret Theony. "Prince wanted to have a place where he could do all his music and make films and do his tour rehearsals . . . under one roof, which back 25 years ago was quite progressive," Theony said.[8]

On September 11, 1987, the production compound officially opened. Prince named his studio Paisley Park after a song on *Around the World in a Day*. From the outside it looked like any large office building, except for the giant glass pyramid that rose up from its top. Prince also launched his own record label called Paisley Park Records. Warner Bros. distributed its albums and helped fund the label. On Paisley Park Records, Prince released his own albums, along with records for artists including Sheila E. and George Clinton.

Inside Paisley Park

Photographers were rarely allowed inside Paisley Park. The few journalists who were allowed inside shared what it was like inside the star's compound.

The huge lobby area had a glass skylight and walls painted with a blue sky and white clouds. Balconies extended out from the second floor. On the first floor were state-of-the-art recording studios, a 12,000-square-foot (1,100 sq m) sound stage, a rehearsal hall, a concert venue, and a nightclub. Upstairs were several production offices, one belonging to Prince. Sometimes he'd sleep there while in the middle of a long recording session.

A trophy room was filled with Prince's gold records and Grammys, along with a secret vault where he kept master tapes of his recordings. The entire complex was topped with a glass pyramid, which glowed purple whenever Prince entered the building.

The Start of Troubles

Prince was on a roll. *Purple Rain*, *Around the World in a Day*, and *Parade* had all produced hits. His next album, *Lovesexy*, took his career in a less positive direction. The naked picture of him on the cover turned off retailers such as Walmart. Many stores refused to stock it on their shelves.

To support *Lovesexy*, Prince launched one of his most lavish and expensive tours to date. Its many-leveled circular set cost $2 million. He spent more than he earned, and the tour lost money. Prince blamed his managers for the dismal returns. In 1989, he fired Fargnoli and installed *Purple Rain* writer-director Albert Magnoli as his new manager.

Batman

As the 1980s drew to a close, Prince produced the soundtrack for the blockbuster superhero film *Batman*. Actor Jack Nicholson, who played the Joker, was a big Prince fan. He convinced director Tim Burton to hire Prince to score the film. Coincidentally, Prince was a huge *Batman* fan. He'd loved the television show and comic book series as a child. The *Batman* theme was one of the first songs he'd taught himself to play on the piano.

The movie was a colossal hit, earning more than $411 million worldwide. Prince's single "Batdance" off the soundtrack soared to Number

▲ PRINCE, *RIGHT*, STARRED IN *GRAFFITI BRIDGE* OPPOSITE INGRID CHAVEZ, *LEFT*.

One on *Billboard*'s Hot 100 list. It sold 1 million copies in just seven days.

GRAFFITI BRIDGE

Prince's next film venture, *Graffiti Bridge*, didn't fare nearly as well. It was meant to be a sequel to *Purple Rain.* The Kid and Morris Day once again played rivals, but this time, they each ran their own clubs. Prince wrote, directed, composed, and acted in it. After its release in November 1990, critics called the movie a failure of career-ending proportions. "We are talking major disaster here, the dynamite that's likely to destroy Prince's increasingly shaky reputation as a pop genius," wrote Richard Harrington of the *Washington Post.*[10] *Graffiti Bridge* grossed only $4.2 million—less than *Purple Rain* had earned in its opening weekend.

The soundtrack for the movie marked the premiere of Prince's new backing band, the New Power Generation. The band was made up of Rosie Gaines and Tommy Barbarella on keyboards, Michael Bland on drums, Tony M. on vocals, and Sonny Thompson on bass. Prince returned to his roots in Minneapolis to scout the members of the New Power Generation from his home music scene. He was looking for a band that could keep up with the increasingly complex sound he would continue exploring throughout the 1990s.

7

Slave

Prince's 1991 album, *Diamonds and Pearls*, was more commercial and successful than his last few efforts had been. The single "Cream" went to Number One in the United States. With this release, Prince returned to his pop-funk roots. Yet critics wondered whether his music was getting too predictable and if he'd lost his groove. "We've heard it all before," complained David Browne of *Entertainment Weekly*.[1]

Prince was also making some questionable business decisions. He spent $2 million to

▸ While promoting *Diamonds and Pearls*, Prince gave a performance at the 1991 International Special Olympics.

produce and promote a pop-rap album for model and dancer Carmen Electra, whom he was dating. Warner hated the record, which didn't produce a single hit song.

The 1991 MTV Music Video Awards

By the early 1990s, Prince's music no longer shocked audiences. Yet his performance at the 1991 MTV Music Video Awards created a stir. Prince sang his single "Gett Off" on a stage lit by columns of fire. He was surrounded by dozens of scantily dressed dancers. The most shocking part came when Prince turned around. He revealed that his yellow jumpsuit had two holes cut out—one over each buttock.

Troubles with Warner

Despite Prince's recent career misses, Warner Bros. still had faith in him. In 1992, Prince put out a press release announcing he and his record company had signed a $100 million deal. It was reportedly the biggest deal in pop music history—more money than Michael Jackson or Madonna had ever gotten. Prince would receive a $10 million advance for each of his next six albums. He'd also get a royalty of approximately 25 percent on each record sold. In addition, Warner Bros. would put $20 million into Prince's own Paisley Park Records label.

Prince continued to produce new music at a furious pace. Despite his epic deal, he kept clashing with his record company. He wanted to release an album every six months. Warner said it could only promote one album a year. "The music, for me, doesn't come on a schedule. I don't know when it's going to come, and when it does, I want it out," he said defiantly.[2]

In 1992, Prince released his fourteenth studio album, titled with only the symbol he would go on to make famous. Radio stations were still playing singles from *Diamonds and Pearls*, so they basically ignored the new record. Five months after the new album was released, it had sold only 1 million copies in North America. Prince blamed his record company for the poor sales. He claimed it hadn't promoted his album enough. Less than a year after Prince had entered into his multimillion-dollar contract with Warner Bros., he wanted out of it. But Warner wouldn't let him go.

Prince met with Mo Ostin and other Warner Bros. executives in April 1993 to voice his concerns. He told them he wouldn't produce any new albums for Warner. Warner could only have music he'd already recorded from his vault of 500 unreleased songs. Ostin thought Prince was just being difficult. But Prince didn't change his mind.

▲ PRINCE PLAYS A CUSTOM-MADE GUITAR IN THE SHAPE OF THE SYMBOL THAT SERVED AS THE TITLE OF HIS 1992 ALBUM.

THE ARTIST IS A SLAVE

On Prince's thirty-fifth birthday, June 7, 1993, he announced in a press release that he was changing his name to the same symbol he had used as the title of his album. "It is an unpronounceable symbol whose meaning has not been identified. It's all about thinking in new ways, tuning in 2 a new free-quency," the release read.[3]

Prince also separated from his band, the New Power Generation.

Prince believed changing his name would get him out of his record deal. It didn't work. He still owed Warner several more albums. The more immediate result of the name change was to cause a lot of confusion among reporters. No one knew what to call him. The Minneapolis *Star Tribune* asked its readers for suggestions. Readers offered names such as "Ambiguity" and "Mysterious Illness." MTV began playing a metallic noise whenever they mentioned him. Finally, a British journalist dubbed him "the Artist Formerly Known as Prince." The name stuck.

The Artist believed his record company had enslaved him by not freeing him from his contract. "The company owns the name Prince and all related music marketed under Prince. I became merely a pawn used to produce more money for Warner Bros.," he said.[4] He began performing with the word *SLAVE* written in black ink across one cheek.

The Artist put out a quick series of albums to fulfill the rest of his contract. *Come* was released in 1993, labeled with the Artist's birth and "death" dates—"1958–1993." Critics considered it a throwaway record, meant to do nothing more

▲ THE ARTIST PERFORMED ON THE *TODAY* SHOW IN 1996 WEARING THE WORD *SLAVE* ON HIS CHEEK.

than fulfill the Artist's contract. *Come* was his worst-selling album to date.

Though the Artist earned more than $10 million a year, he was in financial trouble. He was spending millions of dollars on music and video production. He was also spending up to $6 million a year to keep Paisley Park Studios running. In the midst of their dispute, Warner pulled all funding from the Paisley Park Records label. Financial troubles drove the Artist to close Paisley Park in 1996. Employees were laid off. Clients' studio sessions were canceled.

The Artist finished out his agreement with Warner. He gave them two more new albums and two compilation albums of music he had already recorded. One of the two originals was titled *Chaos and Disorder*. The album did terribly. It barely sold 100,000 copies and fell off the charts after just five weeks.

The 1990s was a difficult decade for the Artist. He battled with Warner Bros. over his artistic freedom. He was nearly broke. And he had become a recluse, withdrawing into the shadows of Paisley Park. "It was the worst period of my life," he said later. "I was being made physically ill by what was going on."[5]

Love and Marriage

One bright spot during these dark times was a new love in the Artist's life. In 1990, he was performing in Europe when he watched a home video that had been sent to him by a 16-year-old belly dancer, Mayte Garcia. He was so entranced with the young beauty he wanted to meet her right away. When they met, the two felt an immediate bond, which they described was as if they'd known each other in a past life. "There's a closeness that you know is right, and you don't argue with," the Artist told Oprah Winfrey during a 1996 interview.[6] The Artist hired Garcia as his backup dancer. The two talked on the phone every couple of days. Within two years, they had started dating.

On Valentine's Day—February 14, 1996—the Artist and Garcia were married in a small ceremony at Park Avenue Methodist United Church in Minneapolis. During their vows, Garcia didn't say her new husband's name. She simply pointed to the symbol-shaped gold pendant around his neck.

Soon after their wedding, Garcia was pregnant. "He was so happy," keyboardist Ricky Peterson said. "I've never seen him happier than when she was pregnant."[7] The Artist wrote the song "Friend, Lover, Sister, Mother/Wife" as a tribute to his wife and unborn baby. He included his baby's

The Artist's Brush with Death

On April 21, 1996, Garcia discovered her husband lying unconscious in his recording studio. He'd been working for three days straight. When her bodyguard tried to wake him, he didn't move. They rushed him to a nearby hospital. It turned out that he had taken a mixture of pills and alcohol. When the Artist woke up in the hospital later that night, he demanded to be taken home. An eerily similar scene would play out almost exactly 20 years later.

ultrasound heartbeat in a song called "Sex in the Summer."

In October 1996, Garcia gave birth to a baby boy. The couple named him Boy Gregory. Just a few days after the birth, Boy Gregory died from a rare condition called Pfeiffer syndrome. The disease made the bones of his skull fuse together too early, which stopped his brain from growing. Not long afterward, Garcia got pregnant again. She lost the second child to a miscarriage.

NPG Records

After Warner Bros. shut down Paisley Park Records, the Artist launched his own label called NPG (New Power Generation) Records. In 1995, NPG put out the single "The Most Beautiful Girl in the World," which he'd written about Garcia. Without Warner to distribute his

An Interview with Oprah

In November 1996, the Artist and his wife, Garcia, sat down with Oprah Winfrey for an interview. The Artist gave the talk show host a tour of their home, showing her the playroom they'd created for their new baby. Although Boy Gregory had died, the Artist talked as though their baby was still alive. "Our family exists," he said. "We're just beginning it. And we've got many kids to have, a long way to go."[8] When Oprah asked a direct question about the health of their son, he said, "It's all good. Never mind what you hear."[9] Garcia later told reporters the Artist had acted that way because he couldn't deal with his son's death. "We had to show people that we were strong, that we had faith, and that we would try again," she said.[10]

▲ In addition to serving as a backup dancer, Garcia, *left*, sometimes recorded vocals for Prince, *right*, in both English and Spanish.

music, the Artist needed help getting his new single to the public. He tried something new, going to independent distributor Bellmark. The company had a hit in 1993 with "Whoomp! (There It Is)" for the band Tag Team. NPG/ Bellmark released "The Most Beautiful Girl in the World" through an 800 phone number. The song reached Number Three on the US charts, making it the Artist's biggest hit since "Batdance" in the late 1980s.

In 1996, the Artist had finally fulfilled his obligations to Warner. Freed from his contract, he officially went out on his own. To celebrate his freedom, the Artist released the album *Emancipation*. He signed a contract with EMI Records to distribute the album, but the Artist set the price and kept the rights to the master tapes. He promoted the record himself with a series of television appearances and radio commercials. And he had full creative control. "There was nothing in the way when I recorded [*Emancipation*]. Nobody looked over my shoulder. Nothing was remixed, censored, chopped down or edited," he said. "This is the most exciting time of my life."[11]

8

EMANCIPATION

During the late 1990s, the Artist largely disappeared from view. He was still working hard behind the scenes, but only his die-hard fans were keeping up with him. Free from the space constraints imposed by Warner, in 1998 the Artist released a three-CD set of previously recorded songs from his vault, titled *Crystal Ball*. It came with an all-acoustic album called *The Truth*.

He sold the box set directly to fans for $50 through his NPG website and the phone number 1-800-NEW-FUNK. The Artist sold

▸ IN THE LATE 1990S, PRINCE SOUGHT OUT NONTRADITIONAL WAYS TO PROMOTE AND DISTRIBUTE HIS MUSIC.

250,000 copies without any ads or music videos. And he kept most of the profits. The direct-to-consumer approach was a new move in the music industry. The Artist set a trend many other musicians would follow in the early 2000s.

A Return to Prince

On May 16, 2000, just before his forty-second birthday, Prince reclaimed his real name after seven years of living under a symbolic one. "I will now go back to using my name instead of the symbol I adopted as a means to free myself from all undesirable relationships," he announced at a New York City press conference.[1] When a reporter called him Prince, he replied, "That sounds great. I haven't heard that in a while."[2]

Artist of the Decade

Prince had been out of public view for several years, but he wasn't forgotten. By the beginning of the 2000s, the music industry began recognizing him as a legend—not just as a musician, but also as a pioneer for artists' rights. In 2000, the Soul Train Music Awards named him Artist of the Decade. Rapper and producer Chuck D introduced Prince by saying, "The man has done more for the freedoms of artists in the last ten years than anyone worth note."[3]

Loss—and a New Love

In the same month he regained his name, Prince lost his love. The double tragedy of losing two babies proved too much for his relationship with Garcia. The couple divorced.

▲ MANUELA, *LEFT*, CREDITS PRINCE, *RIGHT*, WITH INSPIRING HER TO START HER OWN CHARITY, A FOUNDATION CALLED IN A PERFECT WORLD.

On August 25, 2001, Prince lost his father, John Nelson. The two had been distant during much of the 1990s, but they had grown closer in recent years. John had lived in Prince's former home. He had even written songs for a few of Prince's albums.

That same year, Prince met 24-year-old Manuela Testolini when they did some charity work together. They were married on

December 31, 2001, in a secret ceremony in Hawaii. Manuela took Prince's last name, becoming Manuela Nelson.

Prince's mother, Mattie, died soon after, in 2002. During this change-filled period in his life, Prince also found a new spiritual home by becoming a Jehovah's Witness. Prince's new faith quickly became very important to him.

A Comeback

By 2003, Prince had been out of the musical scene for so long that many people thought of him as a has-been. He hired veteran music publicist Ronnie Lippin to help him gain back his popularity. In 2004, he released *Musicology*, his first major album in

Jehovah's Witness

Charles Taze Russell founded the Jehovah's Witness religion in the late 1800s to focus more closely on the Bible's text than other branches of Christianity did. Though Prince was raised a Seventh-Day Adventist, he became curious about the Jehovah's Witness religion when he learned that his friend Larry Graham, bassist for Sly and the Family Stone, was a member of the faith. Prince often asked Graham questions about the religion. By 2001, Prince had converted.

Jehovah's Witnesses are known for going door to door, trying to convert people. Prince's fame didn't exclude him from that responsibility. In October 2003, when a woman named Rochelle opened the door of her home in Eden Prairie, Minnesota, she was shocked to find Prince standing there. Though Rochelle was Jewish, she listened to Prince's appeal for 25 minutes. She

15 years. To support the album, he launched a 63-city tour.

Again, Prince tried a new distribution approach. Instead of simply selling *Musicology* in record stores and online, he gave it away to each fan who bought a ticket to his show. The tour was hugely successful, selling out many venues and helping Prince move more than 630,000 copies of his album. The concert giveaways propelled *Musicology* up the charts and made it his best-selling album in years.

Prince secured his return when he opened the 2004 Grammy Awards with a medley of his biggest hits. He emerged down a purple-lit stairway and performed "Purple Rain." Beyoncé joined him for a duet of "Baby I'm a Star" and "Let's Go Crazy." Prince's five-minute performance is considered one of the greatest in Grammy Awards history.

Prince followed it up a month later, when he was inducted into the Rock and Roll Hall of Fame. He played a stirring guitar solo as part of a tribute to former Beatle George Harrison, who had died in 2001. Prince took the stage along with rock icons Tom Petty and Steve Winwood for a performance that would become legendary. "Prince's breathtaking guitar solo at the end of

▲ CRITICS PRAISED THE DUET PRINCE, *LEFT*, AND BEYONCÉ, *RIGHT*, PERFORMED TOGETHER.

'While My Guitar Gently Weeps' could be the single greatest musical moment at any Rock Hall induction ceremony in its history," gushed Andy Greene of *Rolling Stone* magazine.[5]

Critics also raved when Prince performed during the halftime show at Super Bowl XLI in 2007. Prince's return to the spotlight was hailed as a comeback, although he didn't see it that way. "Comeback? I never went anywhere!" he insisted. "I never stopped playing and recording."[6]

Prince on *American Idol*

During its run from 2002 to 2016, *American Idol* was one of the most popular programs on primetime television. In 2005, Prince made a visit to the show and performed two songs. The star insisted that his visit be a complete surprise—he didn't want any introduction. He went onstage to perform and then left before his name could even be announced.

Divorce and a Move

On May 24, 2006, Manuela filed for divorce after five years of marriage. The press didn't report any reason for the divorce—only that it was Manuela's idea, and it wasn't something Prince wanted.

Since building Paisley Park in the late 1980s, Prince had spent much of his time at the studio. He recorded 30 albums there. Although Prince shut it down in 1996 because of financial constraints, the studio had remained open for private parties and tours. Freed from his financial troubles in 2004, Prince fully reopened Paisley Park. After his divorce, he moved full-time into an apartment in the back of the complex. Paisley Park was where he would ultimately spend his final days.

9

Good Night, Sweet Prince

Though Prince's second marriage had ended in divorce, his career was going strong. Despite his temperamental past, record companies wanted to work with him again. His albums were selling, and his concerts were selling out. Over the next decade, Prince again reigned supreme.

In 2016, Prince launched his Piano & A Microphone tour throughout Australia, New Zealand, Canada, and the United States. In March, he did two surprise concerts in Toronto,

▸ In the early 2010s, Prince once again toured all over the world.

Canada. As usual, the shows were electric and high-energy. Prince was "bouncing around the stage, clapping with his audience, running around the piano. . . . He was having fun," said the venue's CEO, Mark Hammond.[1]

On April 14, Prince played a sold-out show at the Fox Theatre in Atlanta, Georgia. The show had originally been scheduled for April 7, but Prince postponed it because he had the flu, according to his management.

After the concert, Prince immediately headed home to Minneapolis. At 1:00 a.m. on April 15, his private plane made an emergency landing at Quad City International Airport in Moline, Illinois. At first, Prince's management said the stop was due to the flu. But information emerged later that Prince was treated in Illinois for an overdose of the painkiller Percocet.

Prince's Final Show

After canceling his April 7 Atlanta concert because of illness, Prince finally took to the stage on April 14 for two sold-out shows in a row. The tour was titled Piano & A Microphone, which is exactly what fans saw. Prince sat at a baby grand piano surrounded by candles. He put on an hour-and-twenty-minute performance of his greatest hits, plus the song "Heroes"—a tribute to David Bowie, who had died of cancer in January 2016.

Feeling Rejuvenated

Just a day after his emergency stop, Prince was back home at Paisley Park. He biked to a record store to buy Stevie Wonder and Santana albums. Later, he tweeted to his fans that he was "#FeelingRejuvenated."[2]

As if to prove his good health, on Saturday, April 16, Prince hosted a dance party at Paisley Park. Approximately 200 fans showed up. Prince arrived two hours into the party and performed on his new purple Yamaha piano. Responding to fears over his health, he told the crowd, "Wait a few days before you waste any prayers."[3] Blogger Jeremiah Freed later reflected, "The dance party was to show he was all right. When you look back on it now, we should have known that him wanting to prove everything was all right should have been a red flag."[4]

The last time Prince was seen alive was on the night of April 20, when he went to fill a prescription at a drugstore near his compound. Later that night, a member of Prince's entourage placed a call to Dr. Howard Kornfeld, a drug addiction specialist who has a clinic in Mill Valley, California. Kornfeld sent his son, Andrew, a medical student, on a flight to Minneapolis to help. But it was too late.

The End

On the morning of Thursday, April 21, a member of Prince's staff found him unconscious in an elevator at Paisley Park. A call went out to 911 at

9:43 a.m. Paramedics arrived a few minutes later, but they were unable to revive him. Prince Rogers Nelson was pronounced dead at 10:07 a.m. He was 57 years old.

On June 2, the Midwest Medical Examiner's Office released an autopsy report, revealing that Prince had died from an accidental overdose of the opioid pain reliever Fentanyl. Prince had been extremely against drugs throughout his career. He barely drank alcohol. But friends and family revealed he'd taken pain relievers to treat injuries he'd sustained during his concerts, such as hip and knee

Opioid Nation

Prince's death highlighted a growing epidemic of opioid addiction in the United States. Opioids are powerful painkillers, which include OxyContin, Percocet, and Fentanyl—the drug that ended Prince's life. These drugs are safe when used in the correct doses and under a doctor's care. But they can be addictive, and when used in large doses, they can lead to breathing problems and even death.

Starting in the 1990s, doctors began prescribing opioids as a treatment for their patients with chronic pain. Many of those patients became addicted to the drugs and needed more and more of the medicine to find relief. The growing number of opioid prescriptions and increasing dependence on the drugs led to what experts have called an opioid epidemic. Each day in the United States, nearly 80 people die from an opioid overdose.[5] On April 21, 2016, Prince became one of them. After his death, the FBI and Drug Enforcement Agency investigated whether any of Prince's

▲ AFTER PRINCE'S DEATH, FANS LEFT FLOWERS AT FIRST AVENUE.

damage from jumping off pianos while wearing high heels.

FANS, FRIENDS, AND CELEBRITIES MOURN

On the night of Prince's death, thousands of fans converged on the streets around the country. One of the biggest celebrations was a block party held outside First Avenue—the Minneapolis club that had helped launch Prince's career and where he had shot much of the film *Purple Rain*. Many fans carried purple flowers or wore purple clothing. A stage was set up on the street, and musicians such as Lizzo, P.O.S., and Chastity Brown played an impromptu tribute concert. Fans cried, listened to Prince's music, and remembered his contributions to the music industry.

"He was the soul of the music scene of Minneapolis for so many years," said fan Allison Werthmann-Radnich.[6] When the concert ended, fans made their way into the club for the first of three all-night dance parties that would serve as a final farewell party for Prince. Fans danced under purple lights to "Purple Rain" and other hits by the artist.

On April 23, a memorial service was held at Paisley Park. "It was quiet and somber," said Sheila E. "The lights were dimmed. Candles were burning. Just like Prince would have done."[7] Prince's siblings passed out purple boxes containing Prince memorabilia such as T-shirts and tour booklets to fans waiting outside Paisley Park.

Celebrity tributes began pouring in during the days following Prince's death. "Prince opened up my imagination and showed me where I wanted to go as an artist," said Lenny Kravitz.[8] Chris Daughtry tweeted, "We just lost a true artistic PIONEER. Heart broken."[9] Bruce Springsteen

▲ Fans visit a memorial set up on the fence outside Paisley Park in Chanhassen, Minnesota.

opened his April 23 Brooklyn, New York, show bathed in purple light, singing "Purple Rain." The casts of the Broadway shows *Hamilton* and *The Color Purple* also did tributes to Prince.

Dividing Up the Empire

The weeks following Prince's death brought a critical question: What should be done with his recordings and properties, worth an estimated $250 million? And what would happen to the thousands of unreleased live and studio recordings housed in Prince's secret vault? Because Prince didn't have a will to dictate how to distribute his estate, the question would be up in the air for some time after his death.

Prince's one full-sibling, Tyka Nelson, and surviving five half-siblings (John Nelson, Norrine Nelson, Sharon Nelson, Alfred Jackson, and Omarr Baker) filed court documents to share in Prince's estate. Other, more distant relatives, such as a half-niece and half-grandniece, also stepped forward to claim their share of the fortune. Bremer Trust, a banking and investment firm, was put in charge of overseeing the estate until everything was settled, which experts predicted would take months or even years after Prince's death.

Claims to the Throne

Considering the size of Prince's fortune, it's not surprising so many people wanted a piece of the wealth. Prince's sibling and half-siblings were immediately named as his heirs, but many other people also stepped forward to stake their claim. These included Carlin Q. Williams, a Colorado prison inmate who said he was Prince's illegitimate son. A DNA test proved his claim false. Another prisoner, Norman Yates Carthens, said Prince had adopted him and left him $7 million.

Prince's Legacy

In late April 2016, Prince's family announced that Paisley Park would be turned into a museum. Fans would be able to visit and remember his legacy, much as they can at Elvis Presley's Graceland home and museum in Memphis, Tennessee.

Over the course of his four-decades-long career, Prince established himself as a master of many musical styles, from R&B to pop, rock, soul, and jazz. His music crossed racial lines, attracting black and white audiences alike. He had a chameleon-like ability to write songs, play more than two dozen instruments, produce, and act. He was so prolific that the nearly 40 studio albums he produced in his lifetime didn't come close to containing all the music he created.

Prince didn't only write and produce music for himself. He also mentored other acts, helping Sheila E., the Time, Sheena Easton, and other musicians achieve their own dreams of stardom. And Prince revolutionized the business side of the music industry, paving the way for artists to retain more control and ownership over their own music.

By turns an enigma, rebel, and genius, Prince was hard to label or pin down. "He was rock's greatest trickster figure, the trick being that he could become whatever you imagined a rock star to be," wrote journalist Joe Levy.[10] Though his life ended too soon, Prince's musical legacy will live on, undoubtedly inspiring future generations of artists to similarly embrace their own unique styles.

TIMELINE

1958	1977	1978
Prince Rogers Nelson is born on June 7 at Mount Sinai Hospital in Minneapolis, Minnesota.	Prince signs a three-album contract with Warner Bros. Records on June 25.	Prince's first record, *For You*, is released in April.

1982	1983	1984
The album *1999* is released in October; the *1999* Tour starts in November.	The album *1999* goes platinum.	The soundtrack *Purple Rain* is released in June; the film *Purple Rain* comes out on July 27.

1979

Prince has his first Number One hit with "I Wanna Be Your Lover."

1980

Prince appears on *American Bandstand* on January 26; *Prince* goes gold in March; *Dirty Mind* is released in October.

1981

The album *Controversy* is released.

1985

Prince wins three American Music Awards, three Grammy Awards, and an Oscar.

1986

The film *Under the Cherry Moon* comes out in the United States in July.

1987

Paisley Park Studios opens in Chanhassen, Minnesota, on September 11.

1990	1991	1992
The movie *Graffiti Bridge* is released in November.	The album *Diamonds and Pearls* is released.	Prince announces he has signed a $100 million deal with Warner Bros. Records.

2001	2004	2005
Prince marries Manuela Testolini on December 31.	The album *Musicology* is released.	Prince performs on the television show *American Idol*.

1993	1996	2000
Prince announces he is changing his name to a symbol on June 7.	Prince marries backup dancer Mayte Garcia at a Minneapolis church on February 14.	Prince returns to his original name on May 16; Prince and Garcia are divorced.

2006	2007	2016
Manuela files for divorce on May 24.	Prince performs in the halftime show at Super Bowl XLI on February 4.	Prince dies of an accidental drug overdose on April 21.

DATE OF BIRTH
June 7, 1958

PLACE OF BIRTH
Minneapolis, Minnesota

DATE OF DEATH
April 21, 2016

PLACE OF DEATH
Chanhassen, Minnesota

PARENTS
John L. Nelson and Mattie Della Shaw

EDUCATION
Bryant Junior High, Central High School

MARRIAGE
Mayte Garcia: 1996–2000
Manuela Testolini: 2001–2006

CHILDREN
Boy Gregory (with Mayte Garcia; deceased)

CAREER HIGHLIGHTS

Select Albums
For You (1978)
Prince (1979)
Dirty Mind (1980)
Controversy (1981)
1999 (1982)
Purple Rain (1984)
Sign O' the Times (1987)
Lovesexy (1988)
Batman (1989)
Diamonds and Pearls (1991)
Emancipation (1996)
Musicology (2004)

Films
Purple Rain (1984)
Under the Cherry Moon (1986)
Graffiti Bridge (1990)

QUOTE

"The key to longevity is to learn every aspect of music that you can." —*Prince, 2010*

GLOSSARY

alienate
To make hostile, unfriendly, or indifferent.

Apocalypse
The end of the world.

eccentric
Different or unusual.

emulate
To try to equal or excel.

enigma
An inexplicable or puzzling problem, situation, or person.

falsetto
An artificially high-pitched voice, especially in a man.

garner
To get, acquire, or earn.

hydraulic
A mechanical system that is powered by the movement of a liquid.

innate
Born in a person.

longevity
A long life.

new wave
A style of rock music popularized in the late 1970s and 1980s, especially by bands from England.

pseudonym
A fictitious name used to hide one's true identity.

recluse
A person who lives shut up or apart from society.

risqué
Suggestive of indecency. Somewhat improper.

sepia
Dark brown.

silhouette
The outline or general shape of something.

ADDITIONAL RESOURCES

SELECTED BIBLIOGRAPHY

Draper, Jason. *Prince: Chaos, Disorder, and Revolution*. New York: Backbeat, 2011. Print.

Levy, Joe. "Prince." *Rolling Stone*, May 19, 2016. Print.

Nilsen, Per. *Dance, Music, Sex, Romance. Prince: The First Decade*. London: Firefly, 1999. Print.

Ronin, Ro. *Prince: Inside the Music and the Masks*. New York, St. Martin's, 2011. Print.

FURTHER READINGS

Kallen, Stuart A. *The History of R&B and Soul Music.* Detroit, MI: Lucent, 2014. Print.

Marcovitz, Hal. *The History of Rock and Roll.* San Diego, CA: ReferencePoint, 2014. Print.

Robertson, Robbie, Jim Guerinot, Sebastian Robertson, and Jared Levine. *Legends, Icons & Rebels: Music That Changed the World.* Toronto, ON: Tundra, 2013. Print.

WEBSITES

To learn more about Lives Cut Short, visit **booklinks.abdopublishing.com**. These links are routinely monitored and updated to provide the most current information available.

FOR MORE INFORMATION

For more information on this subject, contact or visit the following organizations:

First Avenue
First Avenue & Seventh Street Entry
PO Box 52110
Minneapolis, MN 55402
612-332-1775
http://www.first-avenue.com
First Avenue is where Prince established the Minneapolis sound and recorded the performance scenes in his 1984 film, *Purple Rain*.

Paisley Park Studios
7801 Audubon Road
Chanhassen, Minnesota 55317
952-470-2409
http://www.facebook.com/pages/Paisley-Park-Studios/113351815405479
Prince opened his recording studio in the late 1980s. Since his death, it has become a monument to his music and life. Prince's family has turned Paisley Park into a museum. Fans can take a 70-minute self-guided tour of his concert hall and studios.

Rock and Roll Hall of Fame
1100 Rock and Roll Boulevard
Cleveland, OH 44114
216-781-7625
http://www.rockhall.com
Prince was inducted into the Rock and Roll Hall of Fame in 2001.

Source Notes

Chapter 1. Super Bowl Superstar

1. Vinson Cunningham. "Prince." *New Yorker.* New Yorker, 2 May 2016. Web. 10 July 2016.

2. Christina Capatides. "How Prince's Super Bowl Performance Changed the Game." *CBSNews.com*. CBS News, 22 Apr. 2016. Web. 9 July 2016.

3. Margaret Rhodes. "The Fascinating Origin Story of Prince's Iconic Symbol." *Wired.com*. Wired, 22 Apr. 2016. Web. 4 July 2016.

4. Christina Capatides. "How Prince's Super Bowl Performance Changed the Game." *CBS News.* CBS News, 22 Apr. 2016. Web. 15 July 2016.

Chapter 2. Born to Perform

1. Joe Levy. "Prince." *Rolling Stone*, 19 May 2016. Print. 40–50.

2. Gerald David Jaynes and Robin M. Williams. *A Common Destiny.* Washington, DC: National Academy, 1989. Print. 62.

3. Per Nilsen. *Dance, Music, Sex, Romance.* London: Firefly, 1999. Print. 15.

4. Ibid. 15.

5. Ro Ronin. *Prince*. New York: St. Martin's, 2011. Print. 5.

6. Jason Draper. *Prince*. New York: Backbeat, 2011. Print. 10.

7. Per Nilsen. *Dance, Music, Sex, Romance.* London: Firefly, 1999. Print. 17.

8. Mariel Concepcion. "Trey Songz Shocked at Prince's Visit to *The View*." *Billboard.* Billboard, 10 Dec. 2010. Web. 10 July 2016.

9. Brian Morton. *Prince.* New York: Canongate, 2007. Print. 40.

10. Joe Levy. "Prince." *Rolling Stone*, 19 May 2016. Print. 46.

11. "Prince High School Interview. Central High School." *Prince.org*. Prince.org, 1976. Web. 4 June 2016.

12. Per Nilsen. *Dance, Music, Sex, Romance.* London: Firefly, 1999. Print. 30.

Chapter 3. Record Deal

1. Ro Ronin. *Prince*. New York: St. Martin's, 2011. Print. 25.

2. Per Nilsen. *Dance, Music, Sex, Romance.* London: Firefly, 1999. Print. 48.

3. Ibid. 50.

4. Ro Ronin. *Prince*. New York: St. Martin's, 2011. Print. 34.

5. Stephen Holden. "Prince." *Rolling Stone*. Rolling Stone, 3 Apr. 1980. Web. 16 June 2016.

6. Per Nilsen. *Dance, Music, Sex, Romance.* London: Firefly, 1999. Print. 59.

7. Ibid. 63.

8. Ray Kelly. "Forgotten Concerts." *Mass Live.* Mass Live, 21 Apr. 2016. Web. 16 June 2016.

9. Jason Draper. *Prince*. New York: Backbeat, 2011. Print. 25.

10. Per Nilsen. *Dance, Music, Sex, Romance.* London: Firefly, 1999. Print. 98.

11. "Prince First Ever Full TV Interview! American Bandstand 1979." *YouTube.* YouTube, 26 Apr. 2016. Web. 4 June 2016.

12. Per Nilsen. *Dance, Music, Sex, Romance.* London: Firefly, 1999. Print. 64.

Chapter 4. Rising Star

1. Per Nilsen. *Dance, Music, Sex, Romance.* London: Firefly, 1999. Print. 98.

2. Nathan Brackett. *The New Rolling Stone Album Guide*. New York: Simon, 2004. Print. 655.

3. Jason Draper. *Prince*. New York: Backbeat, 2011. Print. 36.

4. Per Nilsen. *Dance, Music, Sex, Romance.* London: Firefly, 1999. Print. 94.

5. Ibid. 113.

6. Ibid. 117.

7. Ro Ronin. *Prince.* New York: St. Martin's, 2011. Print. 73.

8. Ibid. 75.

Chapter 5. Purple Reign

1. Jason Draper. *Prince*. New York: Backbeat, 2011. Print. 47.

2. Ro Ronin. *Prince.* New York: St. Martin's, 2011. Print. 79.

3. "MTV Premiere Party." *YouTube.* YouTube, 27 June 2014. Web. 28 July 2016.

4. Vincent Canby. "'Purple Rain,' With Prince." *New York Times.* New York Times. 27 July 1984. Web. 29 June 2016.

5. Ro Ronin. *Prince.* New York: St. Martin's, 2011. Print. 111.

6. "Prince and the Revelation." *Paper*. Paper, 31 May 1999. Web. 29 June 2016.

7. Jem Aswad. "Sheila E. Looks Back on Prince." *Billboard.* Billboard, 26 Apr. 2016. Web. 29 June 2016.

8. Jason Draper. *Prince*. New York: Backbeat, 2011. Print. 56.

9. Brian Morton. *Prince.* New York: Canongate, 2007. Print. 117.

10. Per Nilsen. *Dance, Music, Sex, Romance.* London: Firefly, 1999. Print. 155.

11. Neal Karlen. "Prince Talks." *Rolling Stone.* Rolling Stone, 12 Sept. 1985. Web. 29 June 2016.

12. Jason Draper. *Prince*. New York: Backbeat, 2011. Print. 61.

13. Jon Marlowe. "Prince Eyes Concert Lull." *Sun-Sentinel.* Cox News Service. 4 Apr. 1985. Web. 29 June 2016.

CONTINUED

Chapter 6. Highs and Lows

1. Per Nilsen. *Dance, Music, Sex, Romance*. London: Firefly, 1999. Print. 161.

2. Jason Draper. *Prince*. New York: Backbeat, 2011. Print. 63.

3. Patrick Goldstein. "Movie Review: A Misbegotten 'Moon' from Prince." *Los Angeles Times*. Los Angeles Times, 4 July 1986. Web. 2 July 2016.

4. Andrew Unterberger. "Try My New Funk." *Spin.com*. Spin, 28 Apr. 2016. Web. 2 July 2016.

5. Ro Ronin. *Prince*. New York: St. Martin's, 2011. Print. 143.

6. Per Nilsen. *Dance, Music, Sex, Romance*. London: Firefly, 1999. Print. 203.

7. Neal Karlen. "Prince Talks." *Rolling Stone*. Rolling Stone, 18 Oct. 1990. Web. 2 July 2016.

8. Chris Morris. "Inside Prince's Mysterious Estate, the Next Graceland." *Fortune*. Fortune, 26 Apr. 2016. Web. 2 July 2016.

9. Ro Ronin. *Prince*. New York: St. Martin's, 2011. Print. 171.

10. Richard Harrington. "Graffiti Bridge." *Washington Post*. Washington Post, 5 Nov. 1990. Web. 3 July 2016.

Chapter 7. Slave

1. David Browne. "Diamonds and Pearls." *EW.com*. Entertainment Weekly, 4 Oct. 1991. Web. 4 July 2016.

2. Ro Ronin. *Prince*. New York: St. Martin's, 2011. Print. 234.

3. Will Lee. "The Artist, Formerly Known as Prince." *EW.com*. Entertainment Weekly, 4 June 1999. Web. 5 July 2016.

4. Jessica Lussenhop. "Why Did Prince Change His Name to a Symbol?" *BBC*. BBC. 22 Apr. 2016. Web. 5 July 2016.

5. Ro Ronin. *Prince*. New York: St. Martin's, 2011. Print. 245.

6. "Prince and Wife Mayte on Oprah—Part 2/4 (1996)." *YouTube.com*. YouTube, 12 May 2016. Web. 5 July 2016.

7. Ro Ronin. *Prince*. New York: St. Martin's, 2011. Print. 273.

8. "Transcript of the Oprah Winfrey Show." *Prince in Print*. Prince in Print, 20 Nov. 1996. Web. 6 July 2016.

9. Ibid.

10. Charlotte Wareing. "The Tragedy behind Prince's Children—and How He Did Not Acknowledge Son's Death." *Mirror*. Mirror, 21 Apr. 2016. Web. 6 July 2016.

11. Edna Gundersen. "By Any Other Name." *Tulsa World*. Tulsa World, 15 Nov. 1996. Web. 6 July 2016.

Chapter 8. *Emancipation*

1. Kara Manning. "The Artist Is Prince Again." *MTV.* MTV, 16 May 2000. Web. 9 July 2016.

2. "Rare Clip—2000 Press Conference NYC/May 16th." *Facebook.* Facebook, 4 Oct. 2015. Web. 28 July 2016.

3. "Prince on the Soul Train Awards in 2000." *YouTube.* YouTube, 16 Apr. 2016. Web. 9 July 2016.

4. Gary Susman. "Prince Goes Door to Door for Jehovah's Witnesses." *EW.com.* Entertainment Weekly, 15 Oct. 2003. Web. 9 July 2016.

5. Andy Greene. "Watch Prince's Incredible 'While My Guitar Gently Weeps' Solo." *Rolling Stone.* Rolling Stone, 21 Apr. 2016. Web. 9 July 2016.

6. Jeff Jensen. "From the *EW* Archives: Revisiting the Weird, Wonderful Return of Prince." *EW.com.* Entertainment Weekly, 21 Apr. 2016. Web. 9 July 2016.

Chapter 9. Good Night, Sweet Prince

1. David Browne. "Prince's Final Days." *Rolling Stone.* Rolling Stone, 13 May 2016. Web. 9 July 2016.

2. Ibid.

3. Lindsay Kimble. "Prince Asked Fans to Not 'Waste Any Prayers' on Him during Party at Paisley Park Just Days before Death." *People.* People, 21 Apr. 2016. Web. 9 July 2016.

4. David Browne. "Prince's Final Days." *Rolling Stone.* Rolling Stone, 13 May 2016. Web. 9 July 2016.

5. "The Opioid Epidemic." *Department of Health & Human Services.* HHS, June 2016. Web. 9 July 2016.

6. Mallory Simon. "First Avenue: Fans Remember Prince at Iconic Club." *CNN.* CNN, 22 Apr. 2016. Web. 9 July 2016.

7. Joe Levy. "Prince." *Rolling Stone*, 19 May 2016. Print. 50.

8. "Tributes." *Rolling Stone*, 19 May 2016. Print. 55.

9. "Celebrities Express Shock, Sorrow at Prince's Death." *Twitter.* Twitter, 21 Apr. 2016. Web. 9 July 2016.

10. Joe Levy. "Prince." *Rolling Stone.* Rolling Stone, 4 May 2016. Web. 4 June 2016.

About the Author

Stephanie Watson is a freelance writer based in Providence, Rhode Island. For nearly two decades, she has covered the latest health and science research for publications such as WebMD, Healthline, and Harvard Medical School. Stephanie has also authored several books for young adults, including music biographies such as *Elvis Presley: Rock & Roll's King* and *Bruno Mars: Pop Superstar*.

Photo Credits

Cover Photo: Frank Micelotta/Getty Images
Interior Photos: Frank Micelotta/Getty Images, 3; Theo Wargo/Getty Images, 7, 99 (bottom); Mark Duncan/AP Images, 9; Wilfredo Lee/AP Images, 11; Richard E. Aaron/Redferns/Getty Images, 13; Seth Poppel/Yearbook Library, 17; Mark Ralston/Getty Images, 18; Waring Abbott/Getty Images, 20, 27, 96 (top); Gary Gershoff/Getty Images, 23, 97 (top); David Brewster/ZumaPress/Newscom, 29, 32; Jim Steinfeldt/Michael Ochs Archives/Getty Images, 35; Mike Maloney/Mirrorpix/Newscom, 39; Andrew Dunsmore/Mirrorpix/Newscom, 43; Warner Bros./Everett Collection, 45; Warner Bros. Pictures/Everett Collection, 49; Michael Ochs Archives/Getty Images, 55, 97 (bottom); Mary Evans/Ronald Grant/Everett Collection, 60, 64; Jeff Wheeler/ZumaPress/Newscom, 67; Mirrorpix/Splash News/Newscom, 70; Richard Drew/AP Images, 72; Mark J. Terrill/AP Images, 76, 99 (top); Mirrorpix/Everett Collection, 79; Kevork Djansezian/AP Images, 81, 84, 98; mpi31/MediaPunch Inc./IPx/AP Images, 87; ZumaPress, Inc./Alamy, 91; Scott Olson/Getty Images, 93